Sanitation
Workers

Then and Now

Lisa Zamosky

Contributing Author
Jill K. Mulhall, M.Ed.

Associate Editor
Christina Hill, M.A.

Assistant Editor
Torrey Maloof

Editorial Director
Emily R. Smith, M.A.Ed.

Project Researcher
Gillian Eve Makepeace

Editor-in-Chief
Sharon Coan, M.S.Ed.

Editorial Manager
Gisela Lee, M.A.

Creative Director
Lee Aucoin

Illustration Manager
Timothy J. Bradley

Designers
Lesley Palmer
Debora Brown
Zac Calbert
Robin Erickson

Project Consultant
Corinne Burton, M.A.Ed.

Publisher
Rachelle Cracchiolo, M.S.Ed.

Teacher Created Materials

5301 Oceanus Drive
Huntington Beach, CA 92649-1030
http://www.tcmpub.com
ISBN 978-0-7439-9382-1

Table of Contents

Who Takes Your Trash?

Think about the last time you took your trash out to the curb. You probably thought that it would be gone by the end of the day. But, what if you came back to find that it was still there? What if no one ever took it away? What would that be like?

We count on **sanitation** (san-ih-TAY-shuhn) workers to take away our **waste** and keep our streets clean. They have very difficult jobs. Their work is important to all of us.

▼ Trash truck

Trash cans
ready to be
picked up

Garbage Strike

In 1911, there was a **strike** in New York City.
The sanitation workers did not think they
were being treated well. So, they decided
to stop working. Trash started to build up
in the streets.

Waste Management

When workers collect and take away garbage, it is called **waste management** (MAN-ij-muhnt). Sanitation workers mostly remove waste made by humans. Waste can be a solid, liquid, or gas. Gas waste is often what we think of as **pollution** (puh-LOO-shuhn). Dealing with waste in the right way is very important. Waste is harmful to people, animals, and nature.

Mounds of Trash

People in the United States create over 4 pounds (2 kg) of waste per person each day.

▲ Factories create a lot of pollution.

Paper Trail

Sanitation workers pick up a lot of paper. Americans throw away enough paper each year to build a wall 12 feet (4 m) high. And, this wall could stretch across the entire United States!

▲ People sometimes shred paper before throwing it away.

Trash is taken to a dump. There it is taken care of correctly.

Love of Garbage

Rats, flies, and insects love garbage. It is the perfect place for them to live and eat. These pests carry **diseases** (dih-ZEEZ-ez). These diseases can be passed along to people. This is very bad for our health. Garbage must be taken away in a **sanitary** way. If it is not, people are at risk to catch diseases.

Garbage left outside can also attract larger animals. Raccoons like to go through trash. Seagulls are attracted by garbage, too. Even large bears will try to find food in trash cans.

Camping with Bears

If you camp where there are bears, you have to be careful with your trash. Bears look for food anywhere they can. Today, campgrounds have special trash cans. Bears cannot open them.

A bear family looking for food.

YOU ARE IN BEAR COUNTRY!
If this trash can is full, please take your trash with you.

Stopping Diseases

The best way to stop disease is to wash your hands. It is the easiest way, too. Wash your hands before eating or cooking. And, you should always wash them after using the bathroom.

This is a bear-proof trash can.

Getting Rid of Garbage

At one time, pigs were used to control waste. They were allowed to walk in garbage dumps and eat the trash. Pigs got very sick by doing this.

Then, people ate these pigs for their own food. If the pig's meat was not cooked well, people became ill. In the 1960s, people stopped using pigs to get rid of garbage.

Pigs are eating trash at a dump.

Burning trash is bad for the air.

Burning **dumps** was also a way to get rid of waste. This was bad for the air. Disease and air pollution became too common. To change that, the United States had to come up with better ways of getting rid of waste safely.

Baby Waste

Babies use a lot of diapers. This creates a lot of waste. One baby will use about 10,000 diapers! Some people do not want to add to this waste. So, they use cloth diapers. That way, they are not throwing away diapers.

▲ Seagulls eat the trash at this landfill.

Landfills

Sanitation workers began to take waste to **landfills** in the 1940s. These large areas of land are still used today to store waste. Often, the ground is lined with clay or plastic. This keeps the garbage from seeping into the dirt. It also keeps rats and insects away.

Fly Away

Americans throw away a lot of **aluminum**. In three months there is enough to rebuild all of the airplanes in the United States.

▲ Aluminum foil

◀ Benjamin Franklin's great ideas made this country cleaner.

Early Clean Up

In 1757, Benjamin Franklin had a great idea. He started the first public street cleaning service in the United States.

Solid Waste Disposal

In the early 1900s, men carried garbage away in carts. They pulled the carts by hand. Sometimes, horses pulled them. Heavy loads of trash had to be lifted into carts. The work was hard. It was smelly and dirty, too.

Sometimes the job of a sanitation worker is dangerous. They never know what people have put in the trash.

A street sweeper from long ago ➡

◀ A horse-drawn trash cart in 1939

Year Round

Sanitation workers have to be outside all year long. They get very hot in the summer. And, it can be freezing in the winter. How would you like to pick up trash when it is below freezing? Brrr!

Cleaning the Closet

In one year, seven million tons of clothing are thrown away. That's a lot of waste! So, some people hold garage sales. And, some give their clothes to charity.

⬆ Neighborhood garage sale

▲ A dump truck dumps trash in a landfill.

Better Trucks

Later, sanitation workers used trucks to pick up and move waste. Then, **dump trucks** were built. They were used to collect waste. Dump trucks have a bed at the back. The bed tilts backward to dump waste.

In the 1950s, special equipment (ee-KWIP-muhnt) for waste collection was added to the trucks. Workers began using trash **compactors**. These allowed workers to press down trash inside of their trucks. This made room for more trash on the trucks.

Swimming Plastic

Plastic thrown into the ocean is harmful to animals. Plastic kills nearly one million sea animals each year.

⬆ A seagull eating plastic on the beach

◀ Compactors squish the trash. This means trucks can hold more trash.

Modern Equipment

Now, most sanitation workers use trucks with **hydraulic** (hi-DRAW-lik) **lifts**. Trash is lifted into the back of the truck. Workers may not have to leave their trucks to collect waste. This is a big help when the weather is bad.

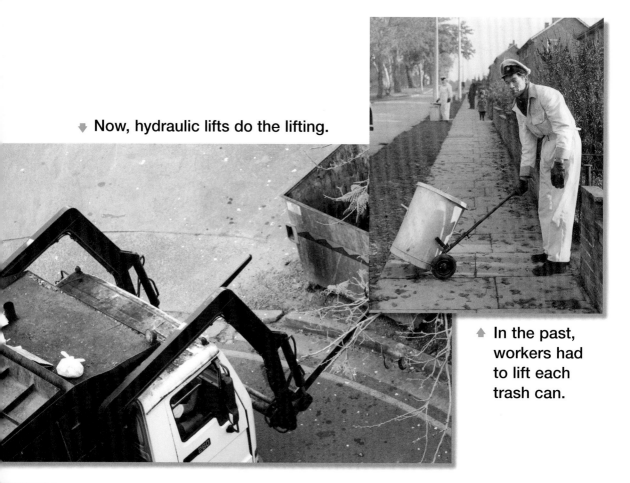

⬇ Now, hydraulic lifts do the lifting.

⬆ In the past, workers had to lift each trash can.

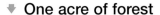 One acre of forest

Living Among the Trees

The average house can take up to one acre of trees to build.

300 feet
(91.44 m)

160 feet
(48.77 m)

One Acre

Write Away

Americans use and throw away 1.6 billion pens each year.

Recycling

To **recycle** (ree-SY-kuhl) means to use something again. Tin, paper, plastic, aluminum, and glass can be recycled. This helps make less trash. If things can be reused, they should not be thrown away.

Recycling is part of waste management. Some communities make it very easy to recycle. You can place your recycling bin outside with your trash. Large trucks come around and pick it up.

It is easy to recycle soda cans, plastic bottles, paper, and glass. Find out how you can recycle at your house. You can help save our planet!

Early Recycling

The first recycling program was in New York City. It started in the 1890s. By 1924, most American cities were reusing some trash.

Soda Cans

A recycled can might be part of a new can within six weeks. You can recycle soda cans as many times as you want.

These plastic bottles are ready to recycle.

Stacks of recycled materials

WE RECYCLE

Important Work

Today, new trucks and tools used by sanitation workers are a great help. But, their jobs can still be difficult. Bad odors and pests are a part of a day's work. They must lift heavy items. And, they have to be careful around dangerous types of waste.

▼ Sanitation workers have helped keep our cities clean for many years.

↑ It is hard work to keep our neighborhoods clean.

What would we do without sanitation workers? Our streets would be dirty. Our communities would be unhealthy places to live. There would be trash everywhere! The work that these workers do helps to keep our neighborhoods clean. And, it keeps us healthy.

A Day in the Life Then

John Walker and the Walker family (early 1900s–present day)

The Walker family is originally from Germany. They **immigrated** (IM-muh-grate-ed) to the United States in the early 1900s. Then, they began working as garbage **haulers** (HALL-uhrz). The Walker family has worked in waste management for 90 years! John Walker started with a horse-drawn wagon. Then, he got a truck. He was the first worker in Portland, Oregon, to use a garbage truck.

John Walker (left) with his garbage truck

This is the Walker family in 1910. ➡
John Walker is in the front row
on the far right.

Let's pretend to ask
John Walker some
questions about
his job.

Why did you decide to be a garbage hauler?

My family came from Germany. We did not speak English at first. This was the perfect job for us. We did not have to know how to speak English to do this job.

What is your day like?

My day is long. The work is hard. We start very early in the morning. Things are a bit easier now that we have trucks.

What do you like most about your job?

When more members of our family immigrate, they come to work with us. We work as a family. I like that we are in charge of our own business.

Tools of the Trade Then

This is a street sweeper from long ago. He had to use a broom and a trash can to sweep the streets. It was hard work!

There were no big trucks long ago. Workers had to pick up the trash using carts pulled by horses.

People used to throw all their trash into metal trash cans. They all looked the same. No one recycled.

Tools of the Trade Now

Today, street sweepers have trucks. The trucks have big brooms on the bottom. This is an easy and fast way to clean the streets.

Now, large trash trucks are used to pick up trash. This has made trash pickup much faster.

Today, many people recycle. They have trash cans that are different colors. Each color trash can is for a different kind of trash.

A Day in the Life Now

Armando Costa

Armando Costa is a sanitation worker in a small town in Minnesota. He drives a street sweeper truck. He helps to keep the streets clean. During the winter, he helps shovel the snow off the sidewalks. Mr. Costa has been working for his community for many years.

Why did you decide to become a sanitation worker?

I have worked as a sanitation worker for a long time. I think my career is a good one. There are many **opportunities** (awp-uhr-TOO-nuh-teez). It is hard work. But, I don't mind that. I like keeping our community clean.

What is your day like?

Lately, it has been snowing a lot. When it snows, I spend most of my time shoveling snow off the streets and sidewalks. This keeps our streets safe for people. Sometimes it gets very cold! I work in the same neighborhood that I live in. My neighbors are very friendly. They bring me hot chocolate to drink when it is cold.

▲ Mr. Costa shovels snow so people can drive on the streets.

What do you like most about your job?

I love to help my community. We live in a great town. I like that with my help, our town stays clean and safe.

This is the street sweeper truck that Mr. Costa drives in the summer. ▶

Glossary

aluminum—a silver metal that is used to make items

compactors—machines that press waste into small packs

diseases—illnesses

dumps—places where waste is left

dump trucks—heavy trucks that have a bed that tilts backward to dump trash

haulers—workers that pick up and move things

hydraulic lifts—truck beds lifted by motors

immigrated—moved to a new country

landfills—places where waste is buried between layers of dirt in the ground

opportunities—chances to do different things

pollution—things that make soil, water, or the air dirty

recycle—to reuse a material

sanitary—free from things that cause bad health

sanitation—getting rid of waste

strike—when workers stop working

waste—trash or garbage

waste management—the business of getting rid of waste

Index

Credits

Acknowledgements

Special thanks to Amy Reaney and the Walker family for providing the *Day in the Life Then* interview.

Image Credits